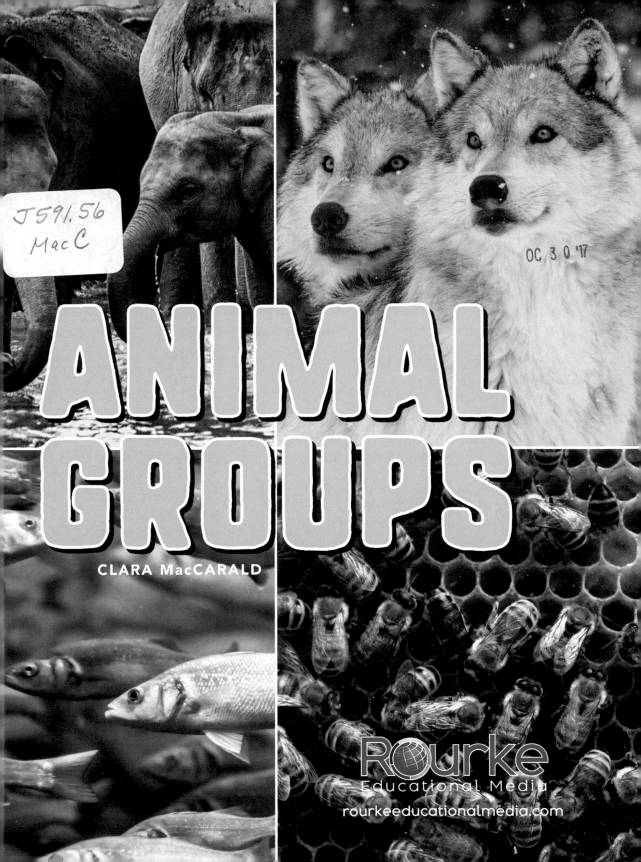

ANIMAL GROUPS

CLARA MacCARALD

Rourke
Educational Media

rourkeeducationalmedia.com

Teaching Focus:
Have students locate the ending punctuation for sentences in the book. Count how many times a period, question mark, or exclamation point is used. Which one is used the most? What is the purpose for each ending punctuation mark? Practice reading these sentences with appropriate expression.

Before Reading:

Building Academic Vocabulary and Background Knowledge

Before reading a book, it is important to set the stage for your child or student by using pre-reading strategies. This will help them develop their vocabulary, increase their reading comprehension, and make connections across the curriculum.

1. Look at the cover of the book. What will this book be about?
2. What do you already know about the topic?
3. Let's study the Table of Contents. What will you learn about in the book's chapters?
4. What would you like to learn about this topic? Do you think you might learn about it from this book? Why or why not?
5. Use a reading journal to write about your knowledge of this topic. Record what you already know about the topic and what you hope to learn about the topic.
6. Read the book.
7. In your reading journal, record what you learned about the topic and your response to the book.
8. After reading the book complete the activities below.

Content Area Vocabulary
Read the list. What do these words mean?

aphid
complex
cooperate
environment
fungus
migration
mobbing
raptors
sentries
species

After Reading:

Comprehension and Extension Activity

After reading the book, work on the following questions with your child or students to check their level of reading comprehension and content mastery.

1. How does being part of a group help animals find food? *(Summarize)*
2. Why might bat mothers want to live in a nursery? *(Infer)*
3. What is one way ants help feed their group? *(Asking Questions)*
4. What groups of animals have you seen in real life? *(Text to Self Connection)*
5. What does it mean for prey to mob a predator? *(Asking Questions)*

Extension Activity

Create a guide to your favorite animals. Research each species. Do they live in groups? How does living in a group help them? For each species you add to your guide, include a short paragraph about them and a picture, either drawn by yourself or printed from the Internet.

TABLE OF CONTENTS

STRENGTH IN NUMBERS

From flocks of birds to schools of fish, nature is full of animal groups. Groups can be small, with two or three members. Or they may be much bigger, with as many as a million members!

A Dolphin by Any Other Name
Some kinds of dolphins seem to have personal names. Individuals use and reply to a special whistle. This whistle was created by the dolphin as a calf.

Some groups endure for a long time. A female elephant lives with her family her whole life, which might last more than 30 years. Other gatherings last for a season, or even a few hours.

Coyotes
Coyotes can live either in groups or alone. Coyotes living in packs protect their family's land, but loners do not. Lone coyotes may someday settle down with a mate.

Groups make life easier for their members. Groups can help each other find food or escape predators. Group members may **cooperate**, or work together, to raise their young. They might teach each other new tricks to survive changes in their **environment**.

Living in groups isn't for everyone. Animals are surrounded by hungry mouths. They must compete for food. Gathering together is not always safer. A large group is easier for predators to find than a single animal. Some animals spend almost their entire lives alone, finding others only to breed.

Although male polar bears spend much of their lives alone, they will sometimes gather and even play together.

FINDING FOOD

Animals of one **species**, or kind, might gather at a food source by chance, since they all eat the same thing. Some animals watch others of their own kind to find food.

Turkey vultures look for other vultures dropping out of the sky because they may have found a dead animal to feed on.

Dinner Bell
Rhesus monkeys don't just call to let other monkeys know food is available. They also communicate how good it is, using either chirps or grunts.

Animals that find a meal might communicate its location to others in their group using body language, smells, or sound. The finder may need help protecting the food, even though it means having to share. Or they may be rewarded later, when a group member brings them to a different meal.

HONEYBEE DANCES

Honeybees communicate the location of flowers with different dances. They use the round dance when flowers are close. They use the sickle dance when flowers are a little farther. They use the waggle dance when flowers are far away.

Sickle Dance

Waggle Dance

Round Dance

WAGGLE DANCE

Honeybees dance to tell others in their hive where to find flowers. The direction the bee waggles, or moves from side to side, tells the other bees in what direction to search. You can try to communicate with dancing yourself!

You will need:

1. A friend
2. An object that can easily be hidden

Directions:

1. Hide the object from a friend in a room or in your yard.
2. Stand in the middle of the area.
3. While your friend watches, face the object and waggle.
4. The friend tries to find the hidden object with no further help.

Did you succeed in communicating the location to your friend? Can you think of other variations? Bees use the length of time it takes to complete one full circle to indicate the distance to the flower.

Some groups share food by storing it. Acorn woodpeckers drill holes into tree trunks. They fill the holes with acorns. During the winter, family members pull acorns from the tree.

Some species of bees store pollen for their colonies, while others turn harvested nectar into honey.

Blood Share
Vampire bats must feed often. But blood doesn't store well. Well-fed bats throw up blood to share with their friends and family who didn't find a meal.

Ants store food, but some species go a step further. They make gardens, which they use to grow a **fungus**. Other ant species have livestock. They tend to a kind of insect called an **aphid**, which is a small insect that sucks sap out of plant stems. The ants guard the aphids from predators and move them from plant to plant. When the ants pet the aphids, the aphids let out sugar water for the ants to drink.

Ants and Aphids

Leafcutter ants feed their fungus gardens using pieces of leaves.

From lion prides to groups of Harris's hawks, many social predators work together to make a kill. Some social spiders build giant webs to catch their victims. Spotted hyenas hunt their own food, but they also gang up to steal another predator's kill. Lions do this too.

Orcas on the Hunt
Orca whales are clever hunters. Pods of orcas surround a school of fish and stun them with their flippers. They also make waves to wash seals into the water.

EYES ON SAFETY

A group of prey has many animals watching for predators. Once a predator appears, being in a group lowers the chances of any one individual being attacked. When a large group flees, the movement confuses the predator and makes it harder to locate a single animal.

Cloud of Confusion
European starlings form dark clouds in the sky for safety. When a raptor, or bird of prey, approaches, the group moves as one to confuse the predator.

GROUP SAFETY

Grouping together can make things easier or harder for prey as they try to stay safe from predators.

You will need:

1. Four or more players

2. A large open area with hiding spots, such as a yard or park

Directions:

1. Make some place in the yard or park the safe spot.

2. One person becomes the predator and the rest are prey. The predator counts to 30 with eyes closed while the prey hides.

3. When the predator finds a hiding place, the prey can run to the safe spot. If they are tagged before reaching it, they have been eaten.

4. When the prey are all either safe or eaten, the game is over.

5. Play again. This time, have the prey hide in groups of two or three.

Were the prey in this game safer if they were alone or if they were in groups?

A flock of European starlings can include more than a million birds.

Many animals sound diffcrent alarm calls for different predators. Vervet monkeys cough at an eagle and bark at a leopard. Hearing the call, other monkeys in their troop know whether to look up or down.

Pronghorn antelopes use smell and their rump patches to warn others of danger.

An Alarming Call
Chickadees are named after their chick-a-dee call, which has several variations. One variation of the call signals danger. The bigger the danger, the more "dees" they add to the end.

In some groups, everyone watches for danger. In others, a handful of animals act as **sentries**. They go on guard, allowing other group members to feed or play.

By standing upright, meerkat sentries can see far around them on the African plains.

Herds of some plant eaters, such as muskoxen, will surround their young members to keep them safe. Wolves can kill a baby muskox, but when faced with a wall of angry adult muskoxen, they're likely to back down.

Crows gang up on all sorts of predators, both in the air and on the ground. This crow is preparing to attack a hawk.

Mobbing is when a group of prey "gangs" up to attack a predator. Small birds often mob **raptors**, birds that eat other animals. Ground squirrels surround and attack snakes, sometimes showering them with dirt and pebbles.

NURSERIES AND BABYSITTERS

Young animals make easy prey for predators, so some parents gather together for safety. Sea otters sometimes form floating nurseries with mothers and babies. Many birds, such as penguins and swallows, nest in large colonies.

Constant Companions
For some young animals, group living means being surrounded by playmates. Play helps social animals bond together while building their skills to fight and hunt later in life.

   Although they nest together, penguins and
swallows don't raise their young as a group.
Individual bird pairs tend to their own offspring.
Lion prides and wolf packs work together in
child-rearing. The mothers feed, protect, or even
babysit each other's young.

Cuckoo bees

Cuckoo bees lay their eggs in the nest or colony of other bee species. In a colony with a queen, the cuckoo bee may kill her and take over.

queen bee

Some animals, such as ants, social bees, and naked mole rats, have **complex** groups. Different individuals have different parts to play. A queen, or two, produce all the young. Workers tend to the queen and her babies. They gather food and protect the group's home.

WEATHERING CHANGE

Grouping together helps animals deal with change. As the seasons change, the weather might turn cold. Food sources may dry up. Some animals take part in an annual **migration**. They move to a place with better conditions. They live there for part of the year before returning home.

Large groups make travel safer and easier. When Canadian geese fly in V-shapes, the geese in front create a wind break. The geese behind them don't have to work as hard. For species traveling on the ground, the leading animals might flatten paths for others to follow.

For animals who stay in one place all year, gathering can be a way to survive bad weather. In North America, flying squirrels share a winter den to keep warm. White-tailed deer gather in deer yards, where many hooves make trails and clearings in the snow.

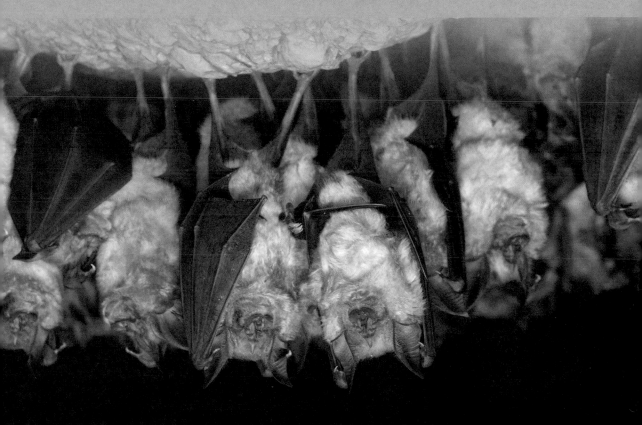

Bats living in colonies huddle together to stay warm when the weather gets cold.

Life also brings unexpected challenges. These challenges force group members to learn new behaviors. Norway rats discover new kinds of food that are safe to eat by smelling what another member of the colony has eaten. Primates learn to use tools by watching each other.

For thousands of years, chimpanzees in West Africa have passed down the skill of making stone tools to crack open nuts.

Smart Thinking!
Tools aren't just for hands. Bottlenose dolphins in Australia have discovered how to protect their nose with a sea sponge while searching the ocean floor for food.

Whether finding food, finding safety, or learning new skills to survive in a changing world, animals find strength in numbers.

GLOSSARY

aphid (AY-fid): a tiny insect that sucks the juices from plants

complex (KAHM-pleks): having many different parts

cooperate (koh-AH-puh-rate): to work together

environment (en-VYE-ruhn-muhnt): a person or animal's surroundings

fungus (FUHN-guhs): a plant-like organism that feeds on other organisms or rotting matter

migration (MYE-gray-shuhn): a seasonal movement to a different region for part of the year

mobbing (MAH-bing): to gang up as a group

raptors (RAP-turs): birds that prey on other animals

sentries (SEN-trees): individuals who stand guard and warn others of danger

species (SPEE-sheez or SPEE-seez): the group to which animals of the same kind belong

INDEX

SHOW WHAT YOU KNOW

1. What is one reason an animal might live alone?
2. How do meerkats stay safe from predators?
3. Why do some ants take care of aphids?
4. What does the queen of a naked mole rat colony do?
5. What are some things animals can learn from other members of their group?

WEBSITES TO VISIT

www.kids.sandiegozoo.org/animals

www.idahoptv.org/sciencetrek/topics/ bird_migration/facts.cfm

www.wolf.org/wolf-info/wild-kids/wolf-families

ABOUT THE AUTHOR

Clara MacCarald is a freelance writer with a master's degree in biology. She lives with her family in an off-grid house nestled in the forests of central New York. When not parenting her own daughter, she spends her time writing nonfiction books for kids.

Meet The Author!
www.meetREMauthors.com

www.rourkeeducationalmedia.com

PHOTO CREDITS: Cover and title page: ©nyiragongo, ©rogertrentham, ©underworld111, ©Christoph Lischetzki; table of contents: ©nattanan726; p.4: ©lemga; p.5: ©Johannes Gerhardus Swanepoel; p.6: ©mirceax; p.7: ©Lynn-Bystrom; p.8: ©Zwilling330; p.9: ©Donyanedomam; p.12-13: ©pxhidalgo; p.13: ©SHSPhotography; p.14: ©jez-bennett, ©RicoChristenson; p.15: ©Debra Wiseberg; p.16-17: ©Schaef1; p.18: ©bobloblaw, ©chas53; p.19: ©pjmalsbury; p.20: ©Alby DeTweede; p.21: ©Bence Mare/Nature Picture Library; p.22: ©Marshall Bruce; p.23: ©earleliason; p.24-25: ©shaunl; p.24: ©Armando Frazao; p.25: ©proxy minder; p.26: ©Michael-Tatman; p.27: ©Cucu Remus; p.28: ©curioustiger; p.29: ©Raquel Bagnol

Edited by: Keli Sipperley
Cover design by: Rhea Magaro-Wallace
Interior design by: Kathy Walsh

Library of Congress PCN Data

Animal Groups / Clara MacCarald
 (Science Alliance)
  ISBN 978-1-68342-347-8 (hard cover)
  ISBN 978-1-68342-443-7 (soft cover)
  ISBN 978-1-68342-513-7 (e-Book)
Library of Congress Control Number: 2017931191

Rourke Educational Media
Printed in the United States of America,
North Mankato, Minnesota